"You will die on the day that you eat"
(Gen. 2:17)

ISBN 9798716706675

1st English Edition: 2021. All rights reserved

Translated by Stavros Raptis

Cover design: Chrysostomos Tromboukis, B.A.
www.chrysostomo.wordpress.com
Edited by Rdr. Symeon Campbell
Publisher: Archangels Publications
Retail orders: www.archangelsbooks.com
Wholesale orders: archangelspublications@gmail.com

FOOD
&
SPIRITUALITY

CONTAINS

SECTION IV

HOW WE FAST

SECTION V

WHEN DO WE FAST ?

SECTION VI

FASTING & HOLY COMMUNION

SECTION VII

THE BENEFITS OF FASTING

SECTION VIII

WHEN WE BREAK THE FAST

SECTION IX

WHEN WE DON'T FAST

PROLOGUE

"You may eat the fruit of any tree in the garden, except the tree that gives knowledge of what is good and what is bad. You must not eat the fruit of that tree; if you do, you will die the same day" (Gen. 2:16-17). Adam ate and (spiritually) died. *"We are what we eat"* (L. Feuerbach). Food, whatever it is, affects our spirituality.

We will see in this book how this mysterious thing happens.

INTRODUCTION

1. BELLY & HEART

"*He* (Jesus) *departed from there ... to a deserted place ... when the multitude heard it they followed Him on foot from the cities"* (Mt. 14:13). They stayed with Him until the evening; they were tired and hungry. They had a great need for a little food; and the Lord fed them with two fish and five loaves (Mt. 14:14-20).

They had until then seen Christ perform many miracles. *"They brought to Him all those who were sick, suffering from all kinds of diseases and disorders: people with demons, and epileptics and paralytics – and Jesus healed them all"* (Mt. 4:24). But the miracle that impressed them was the one that they had just tasted. Two fish and five loaves of bread fed thousands of hungry people! Now they said: *"Surely this is the Prophet who was to come into the world! Jesus knew they were about to come and seize Him in order to make Him king by force"* (Jn. 6:14-15).

If someone is hungry and you give him food to eat, and in fact, whatever is best, you will alter his psychology! If he hated you, he may love you. *"The 'table' and banquet of love dissolve hatred."[1]*

"The journey to the heart passes through the belly." So, when you cast the net of love, you shall easily fish people.

"When you meet your neighbour, honour him with whatever is best. Kiss his feet; kiss his hands; squeeze them; hold them; put them to your eyes, and when the time comes to leave, speak kind words to him; even if he does not deserve it."[2]

This 'typikon' is observed by leaders of various cults to 'attract' followers, especially among young people. They hug them, treat them, speak nicely to them, and they don't simply win them over but convert them into 'weak-willed beings.' The victims reach the point of washing their leader's feet and drinking the wastewater as a blessing...!

When they were with their parents, these very young people were not even inclined to listen to them, even about minor things...!

What do we do as Pastors to fish the sinner from the depths of the sea?

∞ ∞

---

[1] St John of the Ladder, Step 9 on Malice.
[2] Abba Isaac the Syrian, Logos 5

2. CUISINE AND THE BANQUET

It is said that one day Athanasios, the Archbishop of Kazan (1933), was invited to a 'banquet.' As he sat to eat, a fish was served to him. He shouted: *"Don't touch it. It smells. Throw it away!"* What had happened?

The cook had cut his fingers when he was cleaning the fish in the kitchen; he became upset and shouted, *"go to Hell,"*; and the fish was fouled.

Just imagine the 'taste' of the meals cooked with the utterings of obscenities, satanic music, etc.

The same also applies when we take our meals in a sinful environment. It's like eating together with the devil! *"Obscenities (...) summon demons."* [3] Moreover:

Our body emits toxins when we take our meals, swearing at one another. The toxins mix with the food we eat or the water we drink, and the food or water become poisonous. Our grandfathers would say: *"We are eating bitter bread."*

The food, however, becomes tastier when we take our meals with prayers. *"The food that we ate was prepared without oil but was very tasty,"* is surprisingly said by pilgrims to Mt Athos.

---

[3] St John Chrysostom, Homily 32 on the Gospel by John, P.G. 59:187

A charismatic Elder was taking his meal with certain Monks. He saw that some were eating honey, others bread, and others excrement. God explained to him:

"Those eating honey have sat at the table with fear of God, spiritual joy and are praying, and their prayers rise towards God like incense. Those that appear to eat bread are thanking God for the riches that God has blessed them with, and those appearing to eat excrement grumble and say, "this is good, this is not." [4] What do we contemplate when we are eating?

There is a tribe in Africa that kneels and looks to Heaven every time it drinks water, giving thanks to God. Have we ever considered that the water we drink and the food we eat are God's gifts? We are alive due to these gifts!

The Monks in Monasteries wear the same formal attire when seated at the table to receive material food as the attire that is worn when they attend Church to receive spiritual food. They namely take their meals by giving thanks to God, praying *"for You have satisfied us with earthly gifts."*

Our grandparents, who knew what poverty meant, would sit down to eat and say in their prayers: *"God, forgive us since we have food to eat and others don't. Lord, please give them food to eat!"*

Let's think, while we eat until 'our bellies bursts,' others are dying from starvation!

---

[4] Evergetinos, vol. 2, Case 23, Chapter 1

SECTION I
MAN & ANIMAL

1. THE DIFFERENCE

Abba Makarios, the Egyptian, used to say:

"When I was young, I ventured out of my cell and found myself in the desert saying to myself: 'In order to benefit (spiritually), I would ask whoever I met.' I met a young man grazing cattle and asked him:

- Child, I am hungry; what should I do?

- Eat!

- But I have eaten!

- Eat again!

- I have eaten many times, but I am still hungry.

- Old man! Are you perhaps an ass that wants to eat constantly?"

The Abba noted: *"This response was very beneficial to me!"* [5]

And from that moment onwards, he disciplined his stomach even further and became the absolute master of himself.

---

[5] Evergetinos, vol.1, Case 38, Chapter 4

Both man and animal have the same bodily instincts: Hunger, thirst, sleep, and sexual reproduction, which are all for the same purpose: the survival and the propagation of the species. The instinct of hunger leads to the intake of food; thus, the species survives. This also applies to the instinct of thirst, which leads to the drinking of water, and thus the species survives. It also applies to the sexual instinct. *"It is within our nature to spread our seed for the purpose of giving birth,"* [6] etc.

However, the instincts of man are under the control of his mind. In other words, logic intervenes between the personality of man and his instincts. On the contrary, animals are identified by their instincts. This difference makes a man a man and an animal an animal.

For the man, this means inaction. E.g., today, he must not eat before a medical examination. As the hours pass, the instinct of hunger calls out that it wants to be satisfied. However, man used his mind to control the instinct and doesn't eat, despite all the wonderful food that is brought to him.

On the contrary, as soon as the instinct of hunger calls for food, the animal runs for food. The same applies to the sexual instinct. As soon as it calls for satisfaction, it runs to it precisely because it has no mind to control its instinct.

Moreover: Animals do not have passions, malice, and hatred, only instincts. So they move guided by their instincts. For example: If you beat your dog in a moment of anger, the dog will 'forget' and will soon fall at your feet, moved by its instinct. But if you beat your fellow-human, he may even sever all relations with you!

---

[6] St John of the Ladder, Step 27, on Discrimination

Since passions and logic govern man, if he doesn't struggle against his passions, he acts on their basis using his logic. This does not apply to animals since they don't have any logic. This is why man is more dangerous than an animal, no matter how wild that animal may be...!

ങ ✌

2. OUR MIND IS OUR MANAGER

God has placed our manager (our mind) at the highest point of our existence, in the forehead, to oversee our bodies, feelings, desires, and passions. It is *"the Master of the passions"* (4 Macc. 1:7). That implies that it energizes a passion that does not originate from outside but inside the mind.

Eve was defeated by her stomach from the moment her thinking changed; when she looked upon the forbidden fruit from a different view, she *"saw how beautiful the tree was and how good its fruit would be to eat"* (Gen. 3:6), but the fruit itself was the same as before. And the more she looked upon it with this desire, the more her appetite for it increased, and she ate it.

The same thing applies to sexual instinct. The desire stems from inside the mind. That is what the Lord implies when He says, *"there are eunuchs who have made themselves eunuchs* (cut off sexual thoughts from their mind) *for the kingdom of heaven's sake"* (Mt. 19:12).

Let us imagine that your girlfriend is identical to your sister; elegant and slender. She is as attractive as your sister. Now pay attention and see how the sexual instinct functions.

When you look upon your girlfriend, you become tempted. When you look at your sister, you are not tempted. The difference is found inside of you. You look upon your sister with different thoughts. You look upon her as a holy person while looking at your girlfriend as a being of pleasure, as an opportunity *"to make love,"* and are therefore tempted.

However, if you were to look upon your sister with the same thoughts as you look upon your girlfriend, then you would also be tempted by your sister! If you also look upon your girlfriend with the same thought as you look upon your sister, then you would not be tempted by her.

Paul summons us. *"Let God transform you inwardly by a complete change of your mind"* (Rom. 12:2).

"After Noah was five hundred years old, he had three sons, Shem, Ham, and Japheth" (Gen. 5:32). The Bible (according to St John Chrysostom) does not randomly mention that Noah begot children when he was five hundred years old. It demonstrates his great continence[7] while living in a corrupt world, reminiscent of a brothel!

How did he manage?

As a rational being, he employed his mind and didn't blindly follow his nature's every desire.

We are what we choose, and we choose what our 'manager' decides.

CＧ ＢＤ

---

[7] St John Chrysostom, Homily 24 on Genesis P.G. 53: 207

3. WHEN OUR MIND FOLLOWS OUR PASSIONS

"Drowning in a spoonful of water" is a Greek proverb referring to people who are overwhelmed by the slightest. There is only a spoonful of water that is not sufficient for someone to drown! It is our mind that tells us that this minimal amount of water is an ocean! Something similar also happens with our belly.

According to dieticians, the quantity of food that our body requires should fit inside a clenched fist. However, it takes the brain about twenty minutes to receive the message that our belly has received the 'legitimate' quantity. However, in the meantime, our mind intervenes that our belly is empty, *"and the belly cries out for more food, despite being full!"* [8] We eat more and more food until our stomach is about to burst, while animals eat as much as necessary for survival since they have no mind.

St John of the Ladder refers to the belly as a *"cunning lady"*[9] that is always hanging *"over our head!"* So in following its vices, there is a risk of pathogenic dependence upon food. A man can go so far as to eat, be satisfied, induce vomiting, and then eat, and again induce vomiting, and then back to eating!

---

[8] St John of the Ladder, Step 14, on the cunning lady, 2
[9] St John of the Ladder, Step 14, on the cunning lady, 2

He would prefer surgery, an incision to insert the 'ring' that will shrink his stomach, over willing himself to stop eating. God has provided this instinct for survival and salvation, and man turns it into a means for his catastrophe.

The same also happens to the sexual instinct that is stronger than the instinct of hunger. If our belly is a *"cunning lady,"* [10] let us then consider how *"crazy"* and *"cunning"* the sexual instinct can be. In following its vices, there is also a danger of pathogenic dependence! In this case, God has provided this instinct for reproduction, and man has converted it into his catastrophe!

Just as we feel sorry for someone enslaved by their instinct of hunger (eat and vomit, etc.), we should also feel sorry for people (and more so) perverted by the sexual instinct!

Animals compared to humans have a particular 'advantage' here because they have no logic. They don't misuse their natural instincts. Males only "couple" with females and never with males. They use their sexual instinct exclusively for the purpose it has been provided by God, for reproduction and only for reproduction.

Humans may, however, be superior to animals, but when they don't use their logic, they become inferior to animals. It is not enough for him to say that we are 'rational beings'; we need to prove this in practice.

---

[10] St John of the Ladder, Step 14, on the cunning lady, 2

SECTION II
OUR BODY & SPIRITUAL LIFE

1. OUR BODY IS A HOLY TEMPLE

Apostle Paul: *"You do not belong to yourselves but to God"* (1 Cor. 6:19). Have we considered this? So we cannot use ourselves as we think, but as our Owner wants.

"Your body is the temple of the Holy Spirit" (1 Cor. 6:19), which makes your body holy. *"For God's temple is holy, and you yourselves are his temple"* (1 Cor. 3:17). *"We must be careful* (St. Paisios the Hagiorite says) *not to defile the temple of the Holy Spirit. When the Holy Spirit sees that our heart is pure* (it is void of thoughts of carnal sins), *it then dwells within us because It loves purity. That is why the Holy Spirit appeared like a white dove."*

If impure thoughts defile our holy body, imagine how desecrated it is when we commit carnal sins! *"You know that your bodies are parts of the body of Christ. Shall I take a part of Christ's body and make it part of the body of a prostitute? Impossible!"* (1 Cor. 6:15).

So if the Lord took a whip and chased the people selling cattle, sheep, and doves in the Temple (Jn. 2:13-16), which the Jews have built, let us then consider the whip He shall use on those who contaminate the Temple of the Lord which the Holy Spirit built! *"God will destroy anyone who destroys God's temple. For God's temple is holy, and you yourselves are his temple"* (1 Cor. 3:17).

"So then my friends, because of God's great mercy to us I appeal to you: Offer yourselves as a living sacrifice to God, dedicated to his service and pleasing to Him" (Rom. 12:1).

03 80

2. *"BODY OF DEATH"*

"*What an unhappy man I am! Who will rescue me from this body that is taking me to death?"* (Rom. 7:24).

Our soul is hosted in our body and by our body. That implies that the condition of our soul depends upon how the "host" behaves. Anything that the body does influences the soul.

Narcotics, for example, does not flow into the soul but into the body, but they alter the soul's entire disposition. The same thing applies to worldly celebrations. These transform the soul.

That is why St John Chrysostom advises: *"Eat sparingly for otherwise, you destroy the health of your soul."* [11] *"It became the executioner of my soul, by creating providence for my flesh,"* mourns the hymn writer.[12]

Let us not forget that spiritual death entered the soul through the body. *"You will die on the day that you eat"* (Gen. 2:17), God said to Adam and Eve. They ate, and spiritual death entered the soul. The body ate, and the soul

---

[11] St John Chrysostom, Homily on the Holy Pascha P.G. 52: 770
[12] Triodion, 5th Week of Fasting, Wednesday Vespers, Sticheron prosomoion

died, *"your brother was dead,"* the Lord said about the prodigal son who had been enslaved by bodily pleasures (Lk. 15:32). *"They were fat and stuffed with food. They abandoned God their Creator and rejected their mighty savior"* (Deu. 32:15). And it happened so easily. As we see, the easiest way to spiritual death is to become enslaved to the belly.

And Life (Jesus Christ) enters the soul through the body, through corporeal hardships. Apostle Paul: *"At all times we carry in our mortal bodies the death of Jesus, so that his life also may be seen in our bodies."* (2 Cor. 4:9-10). *"I am about to starve"* (Lk. 15:17) said the prodigal son, and this hunger led him to repentance, to Christ!

An Elder stated: *"Someone was riding his donkey. The donkey strayed. The rider took up his rod and beat the donkey, whereby it went back on-course. Along the way, the donkey thought that the rider had lost his rod and again strayed. The rider once again beat the donkey until it went back oncourse. The same also applies to the body. We should temper it with fasting when we stray from God's path".*[13]

C8 80

---

[13] Evergetinos, vol. 2. Case 25, Chapter 9

3. THE THREE STORY HOUSE

Our spiritual and bodily passions are housed in a three-story house within us known as the "tripartite of the soul."

The first floor is the part that leads from the stomach to the area below it. It is the site of the bodily passions: gluttony and sexuality.

The second floor is the central area, the heart, the location of spiritual passions like jealousy, rage, etc.

The third floor is the forehead: the mind, the logical area of the soul. It is the location that regulates the whole of man's substance.

As long as Adam was in Paradise, this three-story house had God as the tenant. His existence was directed upward. In other words, Adam did not eat sensually like a glutton. He ate glorifying His creator. He did not look upon Eve sensually or sexually but as a divine person through which God was glorified.

The same thing applied to his spiritual functions. For example, His anger, his hatred was directed against the devil and never toward his fellow man. The same thing applied to his thoughts. He always glorified God, just like the angels at the throne of God. The expression *"Lord have mercy"* was learned as soon as he left Paradise. When the Lord was transfigured, *"His face was shining like the sun, and his clothes were dazzling white"* (Mt. 17:2). Adam also shone brilliantly in Paradise, but then he sinned.

Before sinning, the house had God as a tenant, and after he sinned, his new tenant was the world. Before he sinned, he instinctively looked heavenward, but he instinctively looked downward toward the world after sinning. He fell from a high level to a low level. That is why this sin is specifically known as the "fall."

Everyone who is born into this world inherits this "fall." Our efforts should be geared to resurrecting this "fall," to rise and look up toward the heavens. And that will happen when the three parts of our soul once again receive the Lord as a tenant.

The first reason for this "regeneration" is found in fasting. *"Elijah was purified with fasting when he saw God on Mount Horeb."*[14] That is precisely why fasting is known as *"the Queen of virtues."*[15]

---

[14] Triodion, 1st week of fasting, Monday Matins, Ode 9
[15] Triodion, Matins of Meat fare Sunday, *"Glory to the Father"* in the 'Praises'

SECTION III
GLUTTONY

1. MEAT & WINE

Adam and Eve did not drink wine or eat meat in Paradise.[16] These entered their world after their expulsion from Paradise.

Eating meat

God created mankind as vegetarians. *"Eat whatever plant grows on the earth, and whatever fruit is borne by the trees"* (Gen. 1:29), said God to Adam and Eve (which is why the human peptic system is the same as the peptic system of herbivores). In sinning, the human states of Adam and Eve altered. They became greedy and were led to eating meat.

They were, however eating meat, in imitation of the carnivores. God acquiesced to their weakness and permitted humanity to eat meat after the flood, but not raw (Gen. 9:3-4) since blood is considered the *"seat of life"* (Lev. 17:11,14).

And since God permits meat consumption, one cannot loathe it because *"for every creature of God is good and nothing is to be refused"* (1 Tim. 4:4).

---

[16] St Basil the Great, Homily 1 on Fasting P.G. 31: 169

The only reason for avoiding meat is due to spiritual ascesis[17], which occurs with monasticism in imitation of the angelic way of life by Adam and Eve *"or in celebration of the new and purified state."*[18]

Drinking wine

Noah 'landed' the Ark on Mt Ararat, planted a vineyard, pressed the grapes, drank wine, and became drunk (Gen. 9:20-21). Noah (says St Basil the Great) was not an alcoholic; he simply did not know about wine since this was the first time he had drunk wine[19] when the others around him *"were eating and drinking!"* (Mt. 24:38).

Consider how much he struggled so that he would not drink even a drop of wine!

The rational use of wine benefits the soul. *"When the earth is watered in moderation, the seed will bear much fruit...The same also occurs with our soul in relation to wine, when it is drunk in moderation: Whatever is planted in the soul shall blossom and grow, bringing forth many fruits. The mind shall remain free of wicked thoughts and carnal desires".*[20]

On the contrary, the irrational use of wine destroys the soul. *"When flooding rain falls upon the ground, caltrops and*

---

[17] Canon 50 of the Holy Apostles & Canon 14 of Ankara
[18] Theodoros the Studite, Doctrina Chronica Monasterii Studii, P.G. 99: 1697-1700
[19] St. Basil the Great Homily 1 on Fasting P.G. 31:169
[20] St Diadochos Fotikes, Evergetinos, vol. 2, Case 18, Chapter 7.

thorns shall spring forth."[21] The same is valid with the irrational use of wine. *"As water rises from the spring, so debauchery springs forth from wine."* [22] *"The passions springs forth like a bee swarm."* [23] *"Where the devil can't go, he sends wine"* (Greek proverb).

Drunkards will not inherit God's Kingdom! (1 Cor. 6:10). And will those who drink a lot of wine without becoming drunk go to Paradise? Prophet Isaiah answers:

"You are doomed! You get up early in the morning to start drinking, and you spend long evenings getting drunk" (Is. 5:11).

෭ ෨

---

[21] St Diadochos Fotikes, Evergetinos, vol. 2, Case 18, Chapter 7.
[22] St Basil the Great, Against intoxication P.G. 31: 499
[23] St Basil the Great, Against intoxication P.G. 31: 460

2. GLUTTONY * HEALTH * DEPRIVATION

St Basil the Great: *"The belly is a very unreliable associate. It may have stored a lot of food inside of it, but what it has retained is harmful and not beneficial".*[24] No matter how much we eat, our mysterious body will only retain what it requires. And what happens to the remainder? A doctor stated: *"9/10 ᵗʰˢ of what we eat goes to the doctors".*

"When a ship (= the "rustic" ships of the old-time) *is transporting a normal load, it can easily sail through the wild seas, but when it is transporting a heavy load, then even the slightest storm can sink the ship. The same also applies to our body: the body does not easily succumb to illness when it eats rationally, which can easily overcome a "storm." On the other hand, it is susceptible to illness when it is heavily loaded".*[25] Accordingly, *"when we are eating, we should stop eating before we are satisfied, regardless of whether we have an appetite to eat more."* [26]

---

[24] St Basil the Great, Homily 1 on Fasting, P.G. 31:193
[25] St Basil the Great, Homily 1 on Fasting P.G. 31:168-169
[26] St Cassian. Evergetinos, vol. 2, Case 18, Chapter 8.

Deprivation adds spices to the food

When we eat the same delicious foods every day, a time shall arrive when we become accustomed to them, and they no longer appeal to us, which results in aversion. The manna from heaven *"tasted like thin cakes made with honey"* (Ex. 16:31). And yet, the Israelites became accustomed to it, and it no longer appealed to them (Num. 11:4-6).

The Bible defines the water that spouted from the rock and sated the thirst of the Israelites (Num. 20:1-11) as *"honey from the rock"* (Ps. 81:16).

The Israelites had been deprived, and when they did drink, they felt that it was as sweet as honey. Being in deprivation, we live in expectation of enjoying whatever has been denied to us! We live in anticipation of something better.

When you offer a piece of candy to a child in Africa, the child will grab it, skip with joy and eat it because the child lives in deprivation.

Do we eat delicious food with the same joy as this hungry child eating candy?

How can we enjoy our food when we cannot comprehend deprivation?

"To hell with easy living" was one of the French students' slogans in May 1968, and they added: *"We want to live."*

The many fasts (deprivations) instituted by the Orthodox Church help Christians enjoy foods that are not suitable for fasting, precisely because they have been deprived. *"Mum! What a nice egg! The cheese is so nice"*, said the young children that had fasted the entire Lent on the eve of Easter.

"As thirst makes water sweet, fasting also assists us in enjoying food. We enjoy whatever we receive that has been denied to us".[27]

Thus, if you want to enjoy your food, just fast!

 CB ❧

---

[27] St Basil the Great, Homily I on Fasting, P.G. 31:176

3. GLUTTONY & ORTHODOX SPIRITUALITY

St John Chrysostom also describes gluttony as a heavy-laden ship of the times. *"Such a ship cannot even be saved by an experienced captain or a calm sea, a lot of sailors or good construction, but is condemned of its own accord. The same happens with those that overindulge in food. Nothing can save them; neither advice nor admonition; neither a fear of the consequences nor a sense of futility. All these are neutralized by uncontrolled eating."*[28]

That is why fasting has the first word in Orthodox spirituality. And this is why we cannot have spiritual life without fasting. *"If a farmer scatters seed over land that has not been properly prepared, he will then reap the thorns instead of wheat, the same applies for us: if we do not "prepare" our flesh by fasting, we will reap thorns."*[29]

A full stomach and an empty soul!

Gluttony & Theology

It is said that a Christian missionary walking through the desert (in Africa) was 'confronted' by a lion! He was afraid...! He kneeled down and fervently prayed: *"Christ! Help this lion think like a Christian to take pity on me and not*

---

[28] St John Chrysostom, Homily 6 on Gluttony, P.G. 50: 770 & Homily 10 on Genesis, P.G. 53:84
[29] St Mark the Ascetic, Evergetinos , vol. 2, Case 19, Chapter 6

eat me,"; and the hungry lion responded: *"Thank You, God! And bless Your servant's meal!"*

We often turn to theology to talk about God. But the issue is, do we speak properly about God? We should consider that perhaps our theological arguments concerning fasting may also stem from our belly. *"It is not the job of everyone, wretches that we are, to theologize. It is not up to everyone to do this. It is not such an unimportant thing"*, said St Gregory the Theologian.[30] And he was criticizing those who started theologizing after taking Holy Communion! [31]

The theology of our Holy Fathers does not 'stem' from rich 'banquets' and comfortable beds but fasting and vigils. *"A mother delivers the belly's pleasing fruit into this world with pain. The pleasant fruit of knowing God and the mysteries of God are born in the soul through the belly's distress".* [32]

With a heavily laden stomach, it is impossible for us to speak about God. *"It is impossible for a fat bird to fly up into the sky. And it is impossible for him who takes care of his body to take theological flights".* [33] *"Heavy food produces fumes which like a cloud envelope the mind."* [34]

Gluttony can even lead to apostasy. *"Jeshurun grew fat and kicked; You grew fat, you grew thick, You are obese! Then he forsook God who made him, and scornfully esteemed the Rock of his salvation"* (Deut. 32:15). That is why one can

---

[30] St Gregory the Theologian, 1st Logos, P.G. 36: 13
[31] St Gregory the Theologian, 1st Logos, P.G. 36: 13-14
[32] Abba Isaac the Syrian, Logos 56
[33] St John the Ladder, Step 26 on the discernment of thoughts, passions and virtues C, 3: 7
[34] St Basil, Homily 1 on Fasting, P.G. 31, 180

discern a denial of Jesus Christ today in the age of body worship.

A proverb: *"Hodja forgot the Koran as soon he saw the halvah."*

☙ ❧

4. GLUTTONY * SEXUALITY * DEVIL

"*They sewed fig leaves together and covered themselves*" (Gen. 3:7). Adam and Eve hid their naked bodies, starting with their genitals, sending the message that the sex is at the center of fallen man!

They first ate the forbidden fruit, and then they had sexual relations (Gen. 4:1). Man is first defeated by his stomach and then by his sexual instincts. The first is followed by the second. *"In the days before the flood people ate and drank, men and women married"* (Mt. 24:38). The Lord links *"ate and drank"* with *"men and women married." "As wood fuels the fire, plentiful food fuels fornication."*[35]

A Monk was besieged by fornication. He pleaded with an Elder to pray for him. The Elder indeed prayed for him for seven days. *"How is the war going, Brother?"* he asked the Monk, completing his prayers.

"It is on-going!" responded the Monk.

The Elder prayed again, and the devil appeared before him as he was praying and said to him: *"I am being sincere with you, I had left him since the first day when you started praying, but that monk has his own demon and is his own worst enemy: He eats a lot, drinks a lot and sleeps a lot!"* [36]

---

[35] Abba Isaac the Syrian, Logos 56
[36] Evergetinos, vol. 1, Case 21, Chapter VI, 5

Another demon said something similar to another Monk. *"There is no reason to bother him since he is one of ours! He eats, drinks...So why should we waste our time? Let's go and torture those that fight us day and night."*[37]

As fasting is a weapon against the devil (Mk. 9:29), so too gluttony is an invitation to him. Thus, the first thing that he seeks to do is occupy our belly. In order to expel Adam and Eve from Paradise, he targeted their belly! He "discovered" that the belly was the weakest link, even with Adam and Eve. He even tried to "tempt" the hungry Christ through the belly by saying to Him: *"If you are God's Son, order those stones to turn into bread"* (Mt. 4:3). He didn't say turn a stone into bread and eat it because you are hungry, but turn all the stones into bread, wanting to thus "tempt" Him with gluttony and saturation.

"The demons dance wherever there is abundance!"[38]

---

[37] Evergetinos, vol.1, Cas 29, Chapter I, 2
[38] St. John Chrysostom Homily 70 on the Gospel by Matthew, P.G. 58: 660

SECTION IV
HOW WE FAST

1. FASTING: AN UNDESIRABLE THING

A Christian was once asked about his favorite passage in the New Testament, and he responded: *"The miracle that Christ performed at the Wedding in Cana"* (Jn. 2:1-11). *"Why?"* *"I like the taste of wine."* If we do not like this miracle, for sure, we will like another (similar) miracle; thousands of hungry people were fed with five loaves and two fish (Mt. 14:20).

Our Crucified Lord is the prototype for our life. Not the great modern idols of hedonism! We have to offer sacrifices to our Lord, starting from our bellies. But narrow is the gate, and difficult is the way which leads to life! (Mt. 7:14). And such a sacrifice is an undesirable thing because hedonism is in our nature!

We don't only want to eat, but we also want to eat well. Nobody likes tasteless food, but above all, nobody wants to be hungry. Just as no one wants to take medicine, even more so, no one wants to go to the hospital.

However, if we need to take medicine and don't take it, our health will worsen. If we need to go to the hospital and don't go, we may then die. There are things in our lives that we don't want, but we have to accept; otherwise, we will be in danger. Fasting is such an undesirable thing. And we need it since we are sick.

Nikos Kazantzakis visited Mt Athos in 1928, where he has an interesting conversation with Makarios Spilaiotis, a well-known ascetic. Below is a relevant extract.

- You lead a very difficult life, Elder; I also want to be saved, is there another way?

- An easier way? The ascetic smiled with compassion.

- A more humane way, Elder!

- There is only one path!

- What's its name?

- Uphill! To ascend a step from satisfaction to hunger, from refreshment to thirst, from joy to pain, to the pinnacle of starvation, thirst, and pain up to where God is seated. The Devil sits at the top of the peak of the good life. It's your choice!

- I am still young. Secular life is also good, and I have time to choose.

The ascetic spread his five bony fingers over my knees and shook me:

- Wake up, child, before Death awakens you!

But he had fallen into such a deep slumber that not even death was able to awaken him.

○₃ ○○

2. FASTING IN THE TRADITION

T he word for fasting in Ancient Greek is derived from the negating particle "νή" and the verb "ἐσθίω" = to not eat. Accordingly, fasting implies abstinence from food. In this way, Christians originally fasted. They either remained hungry all day[39] or tasted something after 3 pm (when Christ expired), a little bread, and a little water (dry rations). Hermas, a disciple of the Twelve Apostles, wrote: *"On the day that you fast, you must not taste anything more than bread and water."*

After the 2nd century, in addition to bread and water, Christians could also eat vegetables.

Other fasting foods were later added, such as olives, fruit and legumes, *"and all invertebrate shellfish"* [40] (seafood without bones). This form of fasting (dry rations) after 3 pm was the most prevalent.[41] *"You wait until the afternoon before you eat,"* St Basil the Great would say to his flock during the period of fasting.[42]

"Those who have fasted and those who have not fasted shall rejoice today" is heard at Church on Easter Sunday.

---

[39] St John Chrysostom, Homily 10 on Genesis. P.G. 53:82
[40] St Theodoros the Studite, Teaching..., P.G. 99:1700
[41] Archim. Vassilios Stefanidis, Church History, 4th Edition, "Astir" publications, 1978, pp. 57-58
[42] St Basil the Great, Homily I on Fasting, P.G. 31:181

Those who have *"fasted"* were the ones that starved during Lent by taking dry rations daily or even every second day! And those who have *"not fasted"* were the ones that ate before the afternoon, a little food that was cooked with or without oil, if they were sick.

This kind of fasting has continued for centuries. *"Many islanders only ate fruit during the fifteen-day fast in August,"* wrote a French Jesuit who had visited the Greek islands during the 19ᵗʰ century.[43]

The American Henry Post visited Greece between 1827 and 1828 and saw our ancestors eating vegetables and olives during Great Lent. He had not seen people fasting with such self-denial anywhere else![44]

The Danish author Hans Christian Anderson also had the same experience during his visit to Greece in 1841. He said: They have a long and strict fast prior to Easter that they do not violate.[45] Peasants, in fact, live on only bread, onions, and water.[46]

---

[43] When Greece was liberated from the Turkish occupation in 1821, the discussions held for establishing the 'Constitution' also considered the issue of placing fasting in the 'Constitution'. They debated whether a decree should be instituted that would compel the Greeks to observe the established fasts. This indicates that fasting was considered an inviolable law even amongst secular circles!

[44] A visit to Greece and Constantinople in the year 1827-1828, Books.go-ogle.com

[45] On Good Friday they would take a little soot (the ash that accumulates in the fireplace 'vent') and mix it with vinegar, as their meal in remembrance of the vinegar that Jesus drank on the Cross!

[46] "A Poet's Bazaar, Pictures of Travels in Germany, Italy, Greece and the Orient", Books.google.gr

This respect for fasting was "alive" until the end of the 20th century. E.g., the Greek soldiers fasted when they fought in the Pindos Range Mountains during 1940. The eyewitness Archimandrite Charalambos Vassilopoulos stated: *"The important thing is that most soldiers observed the fasts, despite the difficulties, even more than the Mt Athos monks!"* [47]

When they broke the fasts, they would exclaim: *"I have been defiled...!"*

03 80

---

[47] Archimandrite Charalambos V. Vassilopoulos, The miracle with the Greeks during Nineteen Forty, "Orthodox Type" Publications, Athens 1980, pp. 126-127

3. PIOUS FAST AND MORE

It is said that a villager so despised a fellow villager that he decided to kill him. Early in the morning, he took his rifle, left the village, went to his fellow villager's field, hid behind a tree, and waited. Lunchtime arrived, and the (candidate) victim had not yet appeared.

His wife thought that (her husband) had gone to tend to the fields and prepared some food and took it to him. Upon seeing the food, the husband started shouting: *"You should be ashamed of yourself! Today is Friday, and you have added olive oil to the food! Do you want to damn me?"*

St. Basil the Great: *"Even though you do not consume meat, you devour your brother with contempt."*[48] *"Let us not restrict the benefit of fasting exclusively to the abstinence from food, since we need also to detach ourselves from all evil, be just, forgive our brother, etc."*[49]

No matter how strictly we fast, unless we fast properly, not only does it not assist us in ascending spiritually, but we are at risk of (with evil in our hearts) *"resembling the worst demons, which never eat."*[50]

---

[48] St Basil the Great, Homily 1 on Fasting. P.G. 31:181
[49] Ibid & Triodion, First week of Fasting, Monday Vespers, Aposticha Idiomelon 1 & Wednesday Vespers, Sticheron Idiomelon 1
[50] Triodion, Cheese Fare Wednesday, Matins, Aposticha

The days of fasting are holy [*sanctified*] because they are dedicated to God and deserve special respect.[51]

In accordance with the Orthodox Church "Typikon" [ritual], it is not permitted for couples to have 'conjugal relations' on the previous evening or even during the day of fasting, even where 'relations' between a couple are sinless. Let us imagine how accountable we are when we commit something sinful on days of fasting!

When for example, certain people went to the Hippodrome on Friday instead of Church to listen to the sermon St John Chrysostom severely reprimanded them! He said that he would not administer Holy Communion to them if they re-offended![52]

Some common queries

In some African and Asian countries, oil, fish, and other products are rare or uncommon. The Christians who lived in those regions couldn't, for argument's sake, fast from olive oil when they didn't have any!

They would then fast from something else designated by the local Bishop, as it was very wisely ruled by the Pan-Orthodox Synod of Crete (2016).

On days of fasting, we would eat olives but not consume olive oil. But doesn't the olive oil come from the olives?

---

[51] Whatever belongs to God (Temple) is known as a 'dedication' [*sanctification*] in the Holy Scriptures (2Chron. 7:9). E.g., *"Judea became His sanctuary"* (Ps. 114:2) since it was God's chosen people; and the Temple courtyard was considered a 'sanctuary' because it belonged to God. The Lord referred to is as *"My Father's house"* (Jn 2:16).
[52] St John Chrysostom, Homily to those leaving the Church, P.G. 56: 268

Olive oil may come from olives, but olive oil is one thing, and olives are something else. Olive oil sustains our body. So, by consuming olive oil, we "subvert" the essence of fasting, which is the pain (denial). For the same reason, they ate grapes but didn't drink wine since wine also sustains our bodies.

Do you consider it as fasting when you overindulge in "fasting" meals? Wouldn't it have been preferable to eat an egg and experienced the sensation of fasting?

Our Church does not permit eggs (and so forth) on days of fasting. Therefore, it is preferable to overindulge with fasting foods than to eat one egg and be hungry. Well, if someone is a glutton, they certainly won't stop at one egg on a fasting day...!

SECTION V
WHEN DO WE FAST?

1. ALL DAY FASTS

The Pharisee said, *"I fast twice a week"* (Lk. 18:12). The Jews (voluntarily) fasted twice a week on Mondays and Thursdays. On the other side, Jesus's disciples didn't fast, and Jesus 'excused' them by saying: *"The day will come when the Bridegroom* (Jesus) *will be taken away from them, and then they* (His disciples) *will fast"* (Mt. 9:15).

When the Bridegroom ascended, His disciples began fasting in His honor. In place of Monday and Thursday, they established Wednesday and Friday. *"We command that you fast on every Wednesday and Friday,"* stated Clement of Rome,[53] the disciple of the Apostle St Peter.

And there was "punishment" for anyone who did not fast every Wednesday and Friday. *"If any Bishop, or Presbyter, or Deacon, or Subdeacon, or Anagnost, or Psalt fails to fast (...) on Wednesday, or on Friday, let him be deposed from office (...) If, on the other hand, a layman fail to do so, let him be excommunicated"* [54].

Fasting on Monday

---

[53] Teachings of the Twelve Apostles. Dideche VIII, 7. & Book 5, Chapter 20, P.G. 1: 904
[54] Canon 69 of the Holy Apostles

During the fasts for Christmas and the Holy Apostles, the Monks also take dry rations on Monday.[55] So this fasting has become an established practice in monasticism (even outside fasting periods).

In days gone by, when reverence was at higher levels, people in society also fasted on Monday. *"We have many examples in secular society where many women in fact fast in exactly the same way on Mondays, Wednesdays and Fridays."*[56]

Eve of Epiphany

Some say that this is the fast for the Epiphany festival, but it doesn't appear to be correct. Fifteen days of fasting for the Dormition of the Virgin Mary, 40 days for Christmas, etc., only one day for Epiphany, and no fasting for the Holy Ascension; how could this be possible?

Some others also say that this fasting is a remnant of the fasting by the Catechumens before Baptism. But why did they fast? In order to receive Divine Grace through Baptism, and we in turn fast on the eve of Epiphany to receive Divine Grace by drinking the Great Holy Water.[57]

---

[55] St Theodoros the Studite, Doctrina Chronica Monasterii Studii, P.G. 99: 1696 - 1697

[56] St Nicodemus the Hagiorite, 'Pidalion', 'Astir' publications 1982, p. 93, Footnotes

[57] Christos M. Enisleidis, The Institution of Fasting, 'Rigopoulos' Publications, 1972, p. 144 & Filio Chaidemenou "Three centuries, one life", Livanis publications, p. 64.

The Elevation of the Cross

Monks fasted in preparation for the Elevation of the Cross (14th September). Some fasted for 14 days, some for 12; others for 4, while people in society fasted on the eve of the festival;[58] until fasting on the day of the festival prevailed.

According to Archimandrite Dositheos, the Abbot at the Holy Monastery of the Holy Virgin at Tatarnis (Greece), the day of the Elevation is a brilliant day, and fasting is not suited to such a day.[59] In days gone by in Russia, they would consume everything on this day. *"It is the supreme day of rest, and everything may be consumed."*[60]

The observation of a strict fast has, however, prevailed. It has now become a 'custom' of the Church, and according to St Basil the Great, 'custom' has the validity of a law.[61]

 C3 &O

---

[58] St Theodoros the Studite, Doctrina Chronica Monasterii Studii, P.G. 99: 1696

[59] Typikon by Saint Savvas, Holy Tatarnis Monastery edition, footnotes to Chapter 12, p. 139

[60] Ibid Typikon D/ski., III, 1528.

[61] *"Let it be said (which is also the most important thing to note) that the custom amongst us which we have to propose in regard to such cases, having as it does the force of a law..."* (Canon 87).

2. GREAT LENT

"*I give you one-tenth of all my income*" (Lk. 18:12), said the Pharisee, which implies that he offered 1/10th of whatever he earned to the Lord (at the Temple). The Great Lent was considered one-tenth of the year, whereby we offer 1/10th of the year to the Lord. *"Annually offering tithes to the supreme King."*[62] We should, of course, devote all our time to the Lord (without a minute or a second for the Devil). This offering should, however, be at its pinnacle during the Great Lent.

Early on the first Monday of Lent (Clean Monday), the town-crier ascended Magnavra Palace and proclaimed throughout Constantinople: *"Observe the Most August and Holy Lent with virtue and fear of God."*[63]

Christians needed to abstain from every secular event. Furthermore, they were not permitted (during Lent) to attend public baths for washing (there were no baths in their houses). *"I am full of scabs and cannot tolerate not bathing,"* they would complain to St John, and he would remain silent! [64] And when certain people attended the Hippodrome,

---

[62] Triodion, Cheese fare Monday, Matins, Kathisma.
[63] Konstantinos Porphyrogennitos, Royal class, 11.27
[64] St. John Chrysostom, Homily Against the inebriated, P.G. 50: 433

St John acrimoniously reprimanded them: *"You have removed the sanctity of Lent from your soul and delivered yourselves into the devil's vices."* [65]

Fasting before Pascha was initially for two days (Friday and Saturday); after the 2nd century, it became one Week;[66] (in imitation of the Jews who fasted for one week before their Passover).[67] Some fasted by eating vegetables, bread and drinking water. There were some who, in fact, fasted (for Easter) even more strictly. They either remained hungry for one day, some for two days, and others for three, four, five, or six days![68]

During the 3rd century, it became forty days, which was an abrupt and huge leap! The early Christians, however, accepted it without any complaints! [69]

Imagine this occurring in our days!

"Everyone should fast on dry rations during Lent." [70] There was "punishment" for anyone who did not fast in this way (dry rations). If he is a priest, *"let him be deposed from*

---

[65] St. John Chrysostom,Homily 6 on Genesis, P.G. 53: 54

[66] Apostolic Decrees, Book 5, Chapter 18, Decree on the Holy Week of Easter, P.G. 1: 899

[67] 2 Chronicles 30: 21-22

[68] St Dionysios, Archbishop of Alexandria, Epistle to Bishop Vasileidis, P.G. 10:1272

[69] They were raised in a climate of 'persecutions'. (Acts 8:1). And the sensation of martyrdom had entered their psychology and they were accordingly willing to suffer for Christ's sake, which is why they didn't have any problems with fasting, no matter how strict it may have been!

[70] Canon 50 of Laodicea

office (...) If, on the other hand, a layman fail to do so, let him be excommunicated" [71].

The first week of Lent is known as the 'Week of Cleanliness,' since they would not eat and drink in as far as it was possible! The fasts for participating in the Pre-Sanctified Services commenced on "Clean Wednesday." *"We do not even receive* (the Host) *until the Pre-Sanctified Gift Service has been performed on Wednesday through traditional fasting."*[72] So we can see that Christians would not even eat a crumb from the Host and 'spoil' the 'three-day period of fasting.'

For the remainder of Lent, they lived by taking dry rations once a day or every second day. *"There are Christians amongst you that compete as to who will fast the most. Some eat a little bread and drink a little water every afternoon, while others don't even do that, but remain completely hungry for two days"*.[73]

This kind of fasting (during Holy Lent) has continued through the ages. *"We even abstain from water during Lent,"* an Orthodox Christian responded to a Roman Catholic Christian (13th century).[74]

---

[71] Canon 69 of the Holy Apostles

[72] Triodion, "Phos" publications 1983, p. 90

[73] St John Chrysostom, Homily 4 on Statues, P.G. 49:68

[74] Konstantinos Giannakopoulos, Professor of Byzantine History at Yale, Byzantium and the West, Translation by Emma Varouxaki, 'Estia' Bookstore, Athens, p. 252

Saturday and Sunday

On Saturday and on Sunday, as resurrection days, fasting (dry rations) is not allowed. *"If any Clergyman be found fasting on Sunday, or on Saturday with the exception of one only* (Great Saturday), *let him be deposed from office. If, however, he is a layman, let him be excommunicated"*.[75] That is the reason why during Great Lent, on Saturday and Sunday, wine and oil are consumed.

Nevertheless, due to the fact that from Monday to Friday, they strictly fasted (dry rations), certain Christians ate cheese and eggs (on Saturday and Sunday of the Great Lent). *"We have likewise learned that in the regions of Armenia and in other places certain people eat eggs and cheese on the Sabbaths and Lord's days of the holy lent. It seems good therefore that the whole Church of God which is in all the world should follow one rule and keep the fast perfectly, and as they abstain from everything which is killed, so also should they from eggs and cheese, which are the fruit and produce of those animals from which we abstain. But if any shall not observe this law, if they be clerics, let them be deposed; but if laymen, let them be cut off."* [76]

 C3 80

---

[75] Canon 64 of the Holy Apostles
[76] Canon 56 of Quinisext

3. HOLY WEEK

Holy Week has been incorporated into Lent until the 10th century. It was then detached from Lent as a separate week that has prevailed to these times. So, Lent ends on Lazarus Saturday (the day before Palm Sunday), whereby *"having completed the edifying Lent"* can be heard through the Churches during Vespers.[77]

The fasting for Holy Week commences on Holy Monday.

Palm Sunday

Certain Monks wanted to lead a more ascetic life during the Great Lent period. So they would leave their Monastery on Clean Monday morning and go into the wilderness for the entire Great Lent and returned on Lazarus Saturday. *"We have been congregated today through the grace of the Holy Spirit"* is heard at the Vespers on Palm Sunday.[78]

They were exhausted from the lack of nourishment and yet continued without nourishment throughout the Holy Week.[79] So in order that they may be able to continue

---

[77] Triodion, Vespers on the Sunday of Lazarus' resurrection, Sticheron idiomelon

[78] Triodion, Vespers on Palm Sunday

[79] St Theodore the Studite, Doctrina Chronica Monasterii Studii, P.G. 99: 1700

standing on their feet until Easter Sunday, they would consume fish at lunch on Plan Sunday. And that is how the tradition of eating fish on Palm Sunday prevailed.

Holy Thursday

St Theodoros the Studite had the following to say about his Monastery: *"Prior to the Service of the Holy Passions* (Holy Thursday night), *we drink a little wine for the ardour of the vigil that will follow."*[80] In society, however, people consume oil *"and thus dishonour the entire Lent."*[81]

The Holy Quinisext Council dealt with this matter and has prohibited the consumption of oil on that holy day.[82] Furthermore:

On the basis of Holy Canon 89 by the Holy Quinisext Council, *"ought to fast until midnight on the Holy Sabbath."* Namely, Christians should remain hungry on Good Friday and Holy Saturday!

It is not proper for us to fill our bellies while our Saviour Jesus Christ is nailed upon the Cross, and He is buried in the Tomb for our sake.

ଓଃ ଓଁ

---

[80] St Theodore the Studite, Doctrina Chronica Monasterii Studii, P.G. 99: 1700

[81] St Theodore the Studite, Doctrina Chronica Monasterii Studii, P.G. 99: 1700

[82] Canon 29 of Quinisext

4. OTHER FASTS

The Christmas fast lasted for seven days until the 9th century,[83] *"apparently as spiritual preparation for Holy Communion."* [84]

When the fasting was extended to forty days, the consumption of fish was permitted (and is allowed) every day except for Mondays, Wednesdays, and Fridays. The fast commenced (and commences) on the feast at the *"Entrance of the Virgin Mary"* (21st November) and ceased (and ceases) on the feast of *"St Dionysios"* (17th December). Since most Christians took Holy Communion on the feast at the *"Entrance of the Virgin Mary"* and at *Christmas,* they abstained from eating fish for one week.

On the evening before Christmas, they fasted without oil, unless it fell on a Saturday or Sunday.[85]

The Fast of the Holy Apostles

This fast is in honor of the premier Apostles Peter and Paul (29th June). It commences on the day (Monday) following the feast of All the Saints (Sunday after Pentecost).

In days gone by, it lasted until the Dormition of the Virgin Mary! It was namely for half of May, all of June, all of

---

[83] Circular to the clergy and laity at the throne of greater Antioch, Patriarch of Antioch, Theodorus Valsamon, P.G. 138: 943-944. & G. Rallis – M. Potlis, Constitution, Holy and Divine Canons, Vol. 4, pp. 420, 488

[84] Vlasios Pheidas, University of Athens Professor, Ecclesiastic History vol. I, 2nd edition, Athens 1995 , p. 963

[85] St Theodoros the Studite, Doctrina Chronica Monasterii Studii, P.G. 99: 1696-1697

July, and half of August. It was a heavy burden, especially after the fast for Lent. The Holy Fathers accordingly restricted it until the feast of Saints Peter and Paul (29th June). [86] *"We observe the Fast of the Holy Apostles, as well as the Christmas Fast; we abstain from oil and fish on Monday, Wednesday and Friday; oil and fish shall be consumed where the festival of the two or Twelve Holy Apostles falls on a Friday or Wednesday."* [87]

The consumption of fish ceases on the (St John the Baptist) Forerunner's Birthday (24th June).

The Fast of the Dormition of the Theotokos

This period was divided into the fasting for the Transfiguration of Our Saviour (1st – 6th August) and the fasting for the Dormition of the Theotokos (7th – 15th August).

Everything was consumed on the feast of the Transfiguration. Some even broke the fast on the following day or even until the Apodosis of the Transfiguration (13th August). Emperor Leon the Wise (741) abolished the consumption of everything that occurred on the Transfiguration by instituting the consumption of fish. [88] Accordingly, the period of 1st – 15th August became a single period of fasting.

---

[86] St Anastasios the Sinaite, G. Rallis & M. Potlis, Constitution, Vol. 4 p. 584

[87] St Theodoros the Studite, Doctrina Chronica Monasterii Studii, P.G. 99: 1701

[88] Christos M. Enisleidis, The Institution of Fasting, 'Rigopoulos' Publications, 1972, p. 123, & G. Rallis - M. Potlis, Constitution, Vol. 4, p. 588

It is a strict period of fasting where oil may only be consumed on Saturdays and Sundays, according to some 'Typika' on the festival in honor of the *"Progress of the Holy Cross."*[89]

Fasts and Sacred Canons

The only fasts that were "protected" by the Canons were those on Wednesdays, Fridays, and Lent.[90] The other fasts were neither "rejected" nor "abolished" by the Canons, because they were introduced later in the Church (11th century).

Accordingly, some people appeared and expressed their doubts about these fasts, which caused a problem in the Church. A local Patriarchal Synod was convened under Patriarch Lucas Chrysovergis's (1156-1169) stewardship during Emperor Manuel Comnenus's reign (1143-1180).

The Holy Synod perceived the unwritten tradition as a sacred "text," as an official ecclesiastical decree, which it was obliged to accept! *"We are compelled to follow the unwritten ecclesiastical tradition and must fast from the first day in the month of August and from the 14th day in the month of November".*[91]

ɔ೩ ೮ɔ

---

[89] Diptychs of the Church of Greece, 2008, "Apostoliki Diakonia tis Ekklesias tis Ellados" Publications, Month of August, p.198, footnote 175
[90] Canon 69 of the Holy Apostles
[91] G. Rallis & M. Potlis. Ibid. , vol. IV, pp. 419-420

5. FASTING FOR SPECIAL CIRCUMSTANCES

Every time that the Jews suffered tribulations, they accentuated their prayer with fasting (=hunger).[92] So when Israel was infected by a plague of caterpillars that ravaged the flora and then by locusts that ate whatever remained (Joel 1:4), the prophet Joel commanded the Israelites to fast (Joel 1:14).

This fasting (for special circumstances) has also entered into the New Testament.

The early Christians who were being led to martyrdom *"remained hungry and without water in the afternoon as they waited for execution with fasting."*[93]

They fasted when they were to be baptized or become a Godparent. *"The person baptizing and the person being baptized fasted prior to Baptism, as well as anyone else that was able to do so."* [94]

They fasted when they were about to assume a ministry in the Church. Before the Apostle St Paul commenced his missionary work, he went into the Arabian Desert (Gal. 1:17-18), where he fasted and prayed.

When the Christians of Antioch sent Saints Paul and Barnabas to the nations: *"Then having fasted and prayed, and laid hands on them, they sent them away"* (Acts 13:3).

---

[92] 2 Chronicles 20: 2-4, Ezra 8:21
[93] Abba Isaac the Syrian, Homily 85
[94] Teachings of the Twelve Apostles. Didache VII,4

Candidates for ordination fasted.

People also fasted when they were about to perform the Sacrament of Holy Unction in their home.

Our grandparents fasted for a week, every time their village went through tribulations (drought, fatal epidemics, etc.), our grandparents held a Divine Liturgy and God performed a miracle.

"I fasted for one week and did not even drink water. God heard my prayers and granted descendants to both my children", a venerable female elder said to me.

Every time that one of their own people died, they fasted forty days for the soul of the departed, especially in Epiros, by expressing their love with pain for the deceased.

SECTION VI
FASTING & HOLY COMMUNION

1. GREAT LENT & HOLY COMMUNION

The early Christians expected the Lord to return in their times (2 Peter 3:4-10). That placed them in a constant state of 'waiting,' whereby they lived an intensely spiritual life (Acts 2:42-43). They began to relax their spiritual struggle when they realized (2nd century) that the Lord was slow in coming. That was the first time when the Christians had spiritually declined.

Unmarried male and female Christians then appeared who applied themselves to strict fasting and praying and aroused their fellow Christians who had fallen 'into decline.' The people respected them and referred to them as 'ascetics' ('temperate').[95]

Accordingly, this temporary decline in spiritual life led Christians of the time to approach Holy Communion in a haphazard manner. St. John Chrysostom informs us: *"Chris-*

---

[95] Archimandrite Vassilios Stefanidis, University Professor. Church History, 4th Edition, "Astir" publications, 1978, pp. 153-1

tians in the past attended the Sacraments without any prep-aration and in fact during the times they were handed down by the Lord." [96]

It was then the first time that fasting was combined with participation in the Holy Eucharist! *"The Fathers saw the damage this was causing and instituted forty days for fast-ing, prayers, sermons and meetings, so that we would be fully purified and take Holy Communion with the cleanest possible conscience."*[97] *"This is the reason why fasting during Lent was instituted"* [98] *"In order to have the leeway for cleansing our sins and thus approach the Holy Sacraments."*[99] *"So we don't fast for Easter or the Festival of the Cross, but for our sins, since we are about to approach the Sacraments."* [100]

Since then, fasting has become the basic prerequisite for participating in Holy Communion. Professor Vlasios Phei-das states: From the 4th century, we find that "repentance and fasting, spiritual meditation and Confession were basic prerequisites for taking Holy Communion."[101]

This slowly became generalized and established throughout the Church and became a Pan-Orthodox un-written law.

C03 80

---

[96] St John Chrysostom, Homily 3, Adversus Judaeos, P.G. 48: 867-868

[97] St John Chrysostom, Homily 3, Adversus Judaeos, P.G. 48: 867-868

[98] St John Chrysostom, Homily 20 on Statues, P.G 49: 197.

[99] St John Chrysostom, Homily 6 on Isaiah, P.G. 56: 139 & Homily 17 on He-brews, P.G. 63: 132

[100] St John Chrysostom. Adversus Judaeos III, P.G. 48: 867-868

[101] Vlasios Pheidas, University Professor, Ecclesiastical History, Volume 2, Athens 1994, p. 910

2. THE PAN-ORTHODOX TRADITION

The fasts of Christmas, of the Dormition of the Theotokos, were originally for seven days,[102] *"apparently as spiritual preparation for the Holy Communion."*[103]

That implies that they fasted for approximately one week when they wanted to take Holy Communion outside these major festivals. *"And where they want to take Holy Communion outside the period of Lent, they should fast for seven days or at least five days."*[104]

They would abstain for one week from meat, dairy products, fish, and three days from oil. They wouldn't even consume oil on Saturday (where they took Holy Communion on Sunday). It is furthermore not coincidental that breaking the fast for fish (during the Christmas fast) commences one week prior to the commencement of the fast (21 November) and ceases one week beforehand (17 December).

Even the Kollyvades movement (18th – 19th century), which fought for continual Holy Communion, would fast on

---

[102] Circular to the clergy and laity at the throne of greater Antioch, Patriarch of Antioch, Theodorus Valsamon, P.G. 138: 943-944.

[103] Vlasios Pheidas, University Professor, Church History, Volume 2, Athens 1994, p. 963

[104] "Interpretation" (Teaching) by Patriarch Kallinikos, approved by the Local Synod of Constantinople, Symeon, Archbishop of Thessaloniki, Complete Works, Rigopoulos publications, Thessaloniki pp. 462-479.

dry rations for one week beforehand.[105] The Venerable Nicodemus the Aghiorite (leader of the Kollyvades movement) advises simple Christians that: *"Those who are able to fast for a whole week beforehand do well."*[106] Even nowadays, the elderly ask the priests: *"Can I take Holy Communion at Easter Thursday if I have eaten fish on Palm Sunday?"*

The decision by the Pan-Orthodox Synod (2016) was based upon this tradition: *"The fast of three or more days prior to Holy Communion relies upon the reverence of the faithful."*

However, we must comprehend it well that we do not partake of Holy Communion because we are worthy, but in obedience to the Lord's commandment: *"Take, eat, this is My Body"* (Mt. 26:26). The Lord is acquiescent towards us so that we do not die spiritually (Jn 6:53). However, that does not imply that we rely upon his mercy and can haphazardly partake of Holy Communion.

०३ ৪०

---

[105] Stylianos Papadopoulos, University professor, St Makarios of Corinth, "Akritas" publications, p. 76
[106] St Nicodemus the Agiorite, Pidalion, "Asteras" publications 1982, p. 230, footnote 1

3. OUR ELDERS AND HOLY COMMUNION

They would say, *"We have taken Holy Communion today,"* when they had experienced an extremely tiring day. It implies that their soul was purified through toil and sweat and they had 'mentally' communed with Christ! They combined Holy Communion with effort, with sweat!

Every time they took Holy Communion, they abstained from fish, dairy, and meat for one week. They also abstained from oil for three days! That was an inviolable law! They would even abstain from water for three days!

The reverent Christians would travel (on 23rd August) by foot (for 15-18 hours) to the Holy Proussou Monastery in Evrytania to venerate the icon of the Virgin Mary, and they would not even consume oil during this arduous trek as they ascended (by foot!) towering mountains! Not even the children consumed oil during this arduous pilgrimage! I recall:

It was August of 1963 when as a ten-year-old child, I first traveled as a pilgrim to the Monastery in the company of fellow townsfolk. On this truly arduous journey by foot, we ate raw tomatoes without oil, some bread and olives, and nothing else. Upon arriving at the Monastery, the reverent Christians attended the Divine Liturgy without even thinking of partaking of Holy Communion since they had not fasted from oil for three days.

"Father, if we drink tea on Tuesday afternoon, can we take Holy Communion at the Service of the Pre-Sanctified Gifts on Wednesday afternoon?" some elderly Christians had asked (in the year 1998) their Priest, Fr. Nikon, from the town of Aneza in Arta (Epirus, Greece). Such a display of respect for the Lord's Body and Blood. Was this perhaps excessive!

Matters have now changed. There is a de-sanctification of everything, even the supreme Sacrament of Holy Communion. St Paisios the Hagiorite said: *"In days gone by, Christians revered the Antidoron more than many monks revere Holy Communion today!"*.

Times may have changed, but Holy Communion is always the same.

☙ ❧

4. HOLY COMMUNION WITHOUT FASTING

According to Canon 66 of the Quinisext, daily Holy Communion without intermediate fasting is only permitted during the week of Easter. Firstly because: The entire week is reckoned as one day, and secondly: It has been preceded by the very strict Lent fast. However, daily Holy Communion during the week of Easter is permitted (according to the Canon) under certain preconditions.

The Canon states: *"Therefore, on the aforesaid days there must not be any horse races or any public spectacles."* In contemporary language, we would say: "Cut out" football matches, gaming, coffee houses, TV, excursions, etc., so that we would have the time and leisure to fully devote ourselves to spiritual matters (and the question is whether we do it?) *"For a whole week, in the holy churches the faithful ought to be free from labor, rejoicing in Christ with psalms and hymns and spiritual songs (...) and applying their minds to the reading of the Holy Scriptures"*; and finally: *"And delighting in the Holy Sacraments."*

However, the majority of Christianity "is fixed" upon the last part and overlooks the previous!

Accordingly, we must understand that the Holy Synod does not recommend daily Holy Communion "haphazardly" but in combination with the total detachment from secular life. *"Therefore, on the aforesaid days there must not be any horse races or any public spectacles."*

It is in combination with complete devotion to spiritual matters throughout Paschal Week. *"For a whole week, in the holy churches the faithful ought to be free from labor."* It implies that the faithful has "passed" the entire period of Lent with dry rations;[107] alternatively, they cannot take Holy Communion.[108]

Is it honorable for Christians to be willing to fast so that they may lose weight and yet be reluctant to fast for Holy Communion?

ॐ ৪০

---

[107] Canon 50 of Laodicea
[108] Canon 69 of the Holy Apostles

5. THE OPPOSING VIEWS.

Some say: *"Why is it that priests can partake of Holy Communion without having previously fasted?"*

Being a member of the laity is one thing and being a member of the clergy is another thing. The priest is required to celebrate the Divine Liturgy regularly or even daily and is accordingly unable to fast or take dry rations for his entire life. On the other hand, the laity is not required to partake of Holy Communion regularly but may even defer Holy Communion until they are ready.

"There is no Sacred Canon that stipulates fasting before Holy Communion."

If a Canon exists that prohibits fasting prior to Holy Communion, you would then be sinning if you fasted since it would be a violation. However, since there is no such Canon, you are not sinning when you fast. Why do you choose not to fast? Is it out of "respect" for Holy Communion or your belly?

The issue is not whether there is a Canon but that we are not disposed to fasting. Do we observe Laodicea Canon 50, which compels us to fast with dry rations throughout Lent? Do we observe Canon 89 of the 6th Ecumenical Council that prohibits us from eating "anything" between Easter Thursday evening and Easter dawn?

The Canons were instituted when a certain problem arose in order to resolve the problem. A problem did not arise in our Church's long-term history regarding fasting prior to Holy Communion since they were already fasting.

Some fasted with the Jews, and a Canon was instituted that prohibited such a fast.[109] Some fasted on Sunday and Saturday, and a Canon was instituted that prohibited that fast.[110] Some scorned at fasting on Wednesdays, Fridays, and Lent, and a Canon was instituted to "punished" them.[111]

"When I observe all the fasts, I do not need to perform any other fasts in order to take Holy Communion."

We are forgetting something fundamental: fasting in the Church implies total fasting (abstinence) or dry rations! The Apostolic Canon 69 "excommunicates" a layperson that does not fast (dry rations!). on Wednesdays, Fridays, and during Lent!

Pay attention to this: We have a situation where a Christian does not desire to strive (fast) before Holy Communion and discourages someone who wants to make this divine effort as if it would harm their soul! While in relation to other sinful matters (e.g., the mortal sin of pre-marital conjugal relations), they are more than likely silent!

---

[109] Canon 70 of the Holy Apostles
[110] Canon 64 of the Holy Apostles
[111] Canon 69 of the Holy Apostles

SECTION VII
THE BENEFITS OF FASTING

1. FASTING: THE MOTHER OF HEALTH[112]

The Orthodox Church's fasts constitute a "guarantee" for our health both in relation to the types of foods that we are permitted to consume and at the time they may be consumed. Professor Antonios Kafatos made the following noteworthy comments:

"A simple recipe for improving our health and reducing the risk of modern illnesses is to observe the fasts of the Orthodox Church. You should fast, if you want to improve your health, even if you are not an ardent follower of religion."

"All of the long-term and arduous conclusions by scientific studies, which have been published in internationally recognized scientific journals, refer to dietary guidelines that coincide with those fasts that have been stipulated and taught by the Christian Orthodox Church for many centuries."

"Strict periodic vegetarianism, which has been stipulated at twice a week (Wednesday and Friday), is particularly valuable for reducing cholesterol and preventing myocardia and certain types of cancer."[113]

---

[112] St Basil the Great, Homily 2 on Fasting, P.G. 31: 193
[113] "To Vima" newspaper, 12/3/1989

Pavlos Toutouzas (Professor and Chairman of the Department of Cardiology of the University of Athens) stated in a lecture (2005): *"If you want to be healthy, don't eat oil on Wednesday and Friday; and adding Monday is a good idea!"*

Even children should fast. Father Vassilios Voloudakis mentions that his children started fasting as one-year-olds. And by the age of three years, they were even fasting from oil while living in the center of Athens![114]

Even pregnant women (without health problems) should observe the Orthodox Church fasts and such cases are not rare!

Some say: *"Everything is contaminated nowadays; the atmosphere, water, food, etc. Large cities are also affected by emissions. Accordingly, fasting is impossible for modern man; that people will fall ill."*

Professor Yuri Nikolaev of the Moscow Therapeutic Fasting Unit supports that this is also why people should fast and even strictly by not eating! In this way, the body can reject the toxins that have been acquired through living in such a contaminated environment.

So we should fast strictly, without fear of falling ill through fasting. We should, in fact, fear the contempt for fasting.

ೞ ಜಾ

---

[114] Fr. Vassilios Voloudakis, Fasting Calendar, 'Ypakoi' publications, 1995, pp. 68-69

2. FASTING: THE QUEEN OF VIRTUES [115]

"*Y*ou must not eat the fruit of that tree; if you do, you will die the same day"* (Gen. 2:17). According to St Basil the Great, this was a commandment for fasting and was, in fact, the first commandment that God gave to mankind![116] *"If it was necessary as a medicine prior to mankind's traumatic-fall from grace, then it is even more necessary after this trauma."*[117]

"Those who are not fasting belong to the enemy's camp. Be careful lest you be proclaimed a deserter because of your belly".[118] On the contrary, *"those who are fasting have been mobilized into Christ's army!"*[119] that is, in the war against the passions, the demons, and sin. Accordingly, there cannot be any spiritual life any spiritual progress without fasting. Fasting is *"the beginning of the spiritual struggles."* [120]

Let us assume that today is Wednesday, and we want to eat something before going to work. Meat, milk, cheese,

---

[115] Triodion, Meat Fare Sunday, Matins, "Glory to the Father" in the 'Praises'.

[116] St Basil the Great, Homily 1 on Fasting, P.G. 31:168

[117] St. John Chrysostom, Homily 5th on Fasting and on the prophet Jonah P.G. 49:307

[118] St Basil the Great, Homily 2 on Fasting, P.G. 31: 188

[119] St Basil the Great, Homily 2 on Fasting, P.G. 31: 188

[120] Triodion, Matins on Cheese fare Sunday, Glory to the Father, in the "Praises"

eggs are on the table, also foods suitable for fasting, such as nuts, fruit, and the like.

And we know that we won't die if we eat nuts, fruit, and the like and won't become immortal if we eat cheese and eggs. Well, what should we do?

If we eat non-fasting foods, it proves that our will is weak, and by eating, our weak will is further weakened. Our will shall be paralyzed when we repeatedly do the same thing on every fasting day, resulting in an inability to resist sin. *"We maintain the same attitude as the dead towards benefits and virtues!"* [121]

If we do not eat, it proves that we have a strong will, and we further strengthen our strong will when we do the same at midday, in the afternoons and evenings, and during every other period of fasting. And with such a will, we acquire the prerequisites for resisting sin, *"tempering the flesh with fasting strengthens the soul."*[122]

This applies to every category of people, especially the young people, whose bodies are "inflamed," whereby fasting is also defined as an *"educator of the young."*[123]

CB 80

---

[121] St John Chrysostom, Homily 10 on Genesis, P.G. 53: 84
[122] St Basil the Great, Homily I on Fasting, P.G. 31: 180
[123] St. Basil the Great. Homily I on Fasting, P.G. 31: 173

3. FASTING: *"VICTORY OVER THE DEMONS."*[124]

*"T*he devil steers clear of incense,"* says a Greek proverb. The proverb does not imply that the devil fears any incense per se, but the offering to the Lord, precisely because it is offered to the Lord. The same also applies to fasting: The devil fears fasting performed in Christ's name and because it is performed in His name (and not dieting for aesthetic reasons). *"This kind can come forth by nothing but by prayer and fasting."* (Mk. 9:29).

"When David fought with the lion, he grabbed it by the mouth and killed it."[125] St Poimen comments: *"We should also restrain our mouth and stomach, by namely avoiding hedonism and gluttony; it is then with God's help that we shall defeat the perceived lion that is the devil."*[126]

An Elder exorcised a possessed person, and the demon said to the Elder: *"Now that you have exorcised me from this person, I will enter you."*
The Elder: *"Come, it will please me."* And the demon entered the Elder, and the Elder began fasting even more

---

[124] Triodion, Cheese Fare Sunday, Matins, "Glory to the Father" in the Praises.
[125] 1 Samuel, 17:32-37
[126] St Poimen, Evergetinos, vol. 4, Case 6, Chapter 6.

strictly. His daily meal consisted of twelve date pits. The result was that the demon could not endure! Then the Elder said to it: *"Hey! Why are you leaving? Stay a little longer!"* And the demon responded: *"Only God has power over you; May he obliterate you!"* [127]

CB EO

---

[127] Evergetinos, vol. 2, Case 15, Chapter 6

4. FASTING AND FORGIVENESS OF SIN

St John of the Ladder talks about a hermit named Stefanos that was an ascetic on Mt Sinai.

He had fallen seriously ill at the end of his life. Shortly before he died, his fellow hermits gathered around him to bid him farewell. His eyes anxiously looked right and left as if he was undergoing interrogation. It was the demons that had come to drive him to despair. They were accusing him of various sins. And the dying man was apologizing: *"Yes, that is so; I have, however, fasted for so many years."*[128]

The remarkable thing is that the hermit used fasting to 'off-set' his sins!

King David had committed adultery and murder. Due to the rigors of his fasting, he said: *"My knees are weak through fasting; and my flesh flails through fatness"* (Ps. 109:24). In enduring such pain and suffering, he said to the Lord: *"Look upon my affliction and my pain; and forgive all my sins"* (Ps. 25:18).

The people of Nineveh fasted and were forgiven and saved (Jonah 3). *"Nothing else contributes so effectively to forgiveness as fasting."*[129]

Moreover, the forgiveness of sins is why the Holy Canons *"impose the obligation"* upon the Priest-Confessor to

---

[128] St. John of the Ladder, Step 7, on the joyful mourning, 50
[129] St Grigorios Palamas, During the time of fasting and prayer, 10

apply strict fasting as 'penance' for sinners[130] because *"repentance without fasting is non-existent."*[131]

"The Angels descend into the churches and document on special lists the names of those that fast" [132] in order to protect them with a greater appetite and disposition![133] This recording only occurs with fasting! For it is precisely fasting that eliminates sin and purifies the soul, something that gives joy to the pure and sinless Angels.

CΆ ΚΟ

---

[130] Canon 1 of the Laodicea Synod, 1st and 13th by St Ioannis the Faster
[131] St Basil the Great, Homily 1 on Fasting, P.G. 31: 168
[132] Homily 2 on Fasting, P.G. 31: 185
[133] St Basil the Great, Homily 2 on Fasting, P.G. 31: 185 & Triodion, Cheese fare Week, Monday Matins, Idiomelon of the Aposticha.

5. "BY PURIFYING OUR HEART..."

"*By purifying our heart with fasting, we shall see Christ.*"[134]

God may have created man from two different elements, body and soul. Still, He did not create two different people, one from soul and another from body, but a unified psycho-somatic being. However, Adam's sin cut that divine creature in half, creating in a manner of speaking a dual personality, two beings, a corporeal (bodily) and spiritual. As a result, spiritual persons have their own spiritual feelings, and corporeal persons have their own bodily feelings.

People of sin choose to satisfy their bodily desires without any concern about wounding the 'other (spiritual) person.' It is like having two children and only feeding one child. But the joy that such people feel is only one-sided since it is corporeal joy.

Humanity's struggle is to unite these two persons to become one united divine being with only one joy, the joy of Christ. "*By purifying our heart with fasting, we shall see Christ.*"[135]

"*Has any 'satiated' bon vivant ever received such gifts?*" [136]

---

[134] Triodion, Cheese Fare Sunday, Matins, Idiomelon hymn
[135] Triodion, Cheese Fare Sunday, Matins, Idiomelon hymn
[136] St Basil the Great, Homily 1 on Fasting, P.G. 31: 180

The entire life of all our Church's saints was a lifelong Great Lent. They were, namely, hungry throughout their lives.[137]

Certain Saints did not even eat that minimal food in their struggle against the sinless and unavoidable pleasure that every person derives when the instinct of hunger is satisfied. *"Abba Pior ate while walking; when someone once asked him: 'why do you eat like that?' he responded: 'So my soul does not sense corporeal satisfaction as I am eating'".*[138] Saint Akakios of Mt Athos mixed wild and dry greens (his daily food) with ash, which he personally made by grinding stones. And God blessed him. His relics were fragrant....![139]

They did not have a body of steel but an iron will!

All the above imply that only the Orthodox Church 'produces' saints since only the Orthodox Christians have so many and strict fasts (in the name of Christ), which are a necessary prerequisite for sanctification.

ল৪ ৪০

---

[137] In the lives of the Saints we may read that certain Monks broke the fast when they accepted visitors. This doesn't imply that they consumed oil, eggs and meat. Since the visitors were on-foot, instead of taking dry rations at three in the afternoon, they took dry rations earlier; or they may have steamed some lentils or a few beans, but only thus far. Let us not *"judge others by our own standards"*.

[138] Gerontikon, Abba Pior, 2

[139] Megas Synaxaristis of the Orthodox Church, Vol. 4, Edition 3, Athens 1981, p. 220

6. PRIEST & FASTING

The Church "Typikon" compels the Priest to be abstinent (before the Divine Liturgy) *"from the evening"* [before] and in fact 'in all matters.' In this way, *"the supplications on behalf of the people are acceptable to God."*[140]

"Do not drink wine and strong drink ... when you go into the Tabernacle of Testimony or when you approach the altar, lest you die" (Lev. 10:9). *"And if they prepared themselves in this manner in order to sacrifice goats and calves, then how should we prepare ourselves who 'touch' and sacrifice the Son of God?."*[141] *"It is not possible to attempt priestly functions without fasting,"* says St Basil the Great.[142]

Note the difference: *"Fasting sanctifies the Monk while perfecting the Priest,"*[143] since the Priest is already sanctified by the holy Priesthood and becomes perfect by fasting.

---

[140] Canon 13 of the Quinisext Council & Canons 3 & 4 of the Council of Carthage

[141] St John Chrysostom, Homily 3 on the Epistle to the Ephesians, P.G. 62: 28

[142] St Basil the Great, Homily I on Fasting, P.G. 31: 172

[143] St Basil the Great, Homily I on Fasting, P.G. 31: 172

As the guide of the people, the Priest is required to observe the fasts of the Church.[144] *"An army comprised of lions that is led by an elephant is never an army of lions,"* was meaningfully stated by Napoleon the Great. Truly:

What shall our excuse be when we don't even discuss fasting with our people? Have we reckoned the magnitude of our sin when our people ignore the divine law of fasting? For we are responsible for not just one soul but the entire congregation.

On the contrary, when we inspire our spiritual children to observe the fasting, we will receive great mercy from the merciful God!

No one respects a well-fed Priest (and even a lay Christian!) Their lips may say, *"it is proper to eat,"* but their heart ridicules him!

A proverb: *"The innkeeper may love the alcoholic but will not consider him for a son-in-law."*

---

[144] More: Canon 69 of the Holy Apostles; St Nikephoros, Patriarch of Constantinople; Rallis, G. and Potlis, M., Constitution, Vol. 4. p. 431, Question 3 *"what is the purpose of fasting in August"*, Nikolaos, Patriarch of Constantinople, Rallis, G. and Potlis, M., Constitution, Vol. 4 p. 420

SECTION VIII
WHEN WE BREAK THE FAST

1. CONSUMPTION OF OIL AND FISH

Oil and fish are consumed on the feast of Saints. That, however, was not always the case. There were two "Typika" until the 12th century.

One "Typikon" mentions that we stop working ('lay day') on the feasts of Saints, where oil and or fish was consumed, and the other "Typikon" only mentions a 'lay day.'

That created confusion amongst the Christians; the confusion was subsequently conveyed to the Mt Athos Monasteries. The Monks sent (1111) a letter to the Patriarch of Constantinople, Nikolaos III.

The Patriarch relied upon Canon 69 of the Holy Apostles and responded: *"the faithful should fast on every Wednesday and Friday; only illness can be an impediment... The fast shall not be broken on the festivals of Saints..."* [145]

The consumption of oil or even fish ultimately prevailed on the feast of Saints.

Consumption of oil is permitted on the feasts of the major Saints and Martyrs. The solitary exception is the feast of St John the Baptist (29th August).

---

[145] Varrioum note, P.G: 1: 05

"We shall consume wine and oil until the performance (Apodosis) *of the festival"* is mentioned in the D/ski Typikon[146] regarding the feast at the Elevation of the Cross. So, we find that some local "Typika" permit the consumption of oil on the intervening Wednesdays and Fridays until the Apodosis of Epiphany, Presentation of Our Lord, Pascha,[147] Assumption, and Dormition of the Virgin Mary. And where we are living in the atmosphere of these feasts, it is not wrong to consume oil until their Apodosis.

Consumption of fish is permitted at the great feasts of the *"Transfiguration of the Saviour," "Annunciation,"* and *"Palm Sunday"* because they coincide with fasting periods. Everything they would 'fall on' Wednesdays and Fridays outside the fasting periods.

Fish may also be consumed:

At the feast of Saints Peter and Paul (29th June); at the 'Synaxis' (7th January) of St John the Baptist, and on his Birthday (24th June); and especially on the feasts of the Virgin Mary: Birthday (8th September), Entrance into the Temple (21st November), the Presentation of Our Lord at the Temple, (2nd February) and at the Dormition (15th August), which is also the leading feast.

It should be noted that the consumption of everything is not even permitted on the leading feast at the Dormition of the Virgin Mary so that we do not forget the Crucifixion of the Lord.

---

[146] 1528 Typikon, D/ski III, from the book: Typikon by St Savvas, Holy Tatarnis Monastery Publications, footnotes to Chapter 12, p. 139
[147] St Theodoros the Studite, Doctrina Chronica Monasterii Studii, P.G. 99: 1700

Just imagine the magnitude of our sin when we break these established fasts on Wednesdays and Fridays without good reasons.

ෲ ෴

2. CONSUMPTION OF EVERYTHING

It is permitted on the Feasts of Jesus Christ (outside the fasting periods). There was, however, a problem regarding the festival of Epiphany.

Christmas and Epiphany were celebrated together until around the mid-4th century. When these feasts were separated, the issue arose whether consumption of everything should be permitted on both the feasts.[148]

This issue was also conveyed to the Mt Athos Monasteries, whereby the Monks also raised this question with Patriarch Nikolaos III. The Patriarch responded: *"It is sufficient for us to consume oil and fish during the customary fast on these days, in accordance with Canon 69 of the Holy Apostles"* (since they arrived at the consumption of fish from dry-rations or total abstinence). *"The consumption of meat or cheese is a poor argument in favor of gluttony, which has not been decreed by Apostolic Canon 'The Kingdom of God is not about eating and drinking' and the following."*[149]

The consumption of everything ultimately prevailed.

Fish was consumed at the feast of Mid-Pentecost. However, it is a Feast of Jesus Christ that must be noted falls during the brilliant period of Pentecost, and accordingly, everything must be allowed to be consumed.

---

[148] St Theodoros the Studite, Doctrina Chronica Monasterii Studii, P.G. 99: 1697
[149] Varrioum note, P.G. 1: 906

And upon these additional grounds, this feast cannot be equated to the feast in honor of Saints where the consumption of fish is permitted. Saint Theodoros the Studite signifies the consumption of everything.[150]

Consumption of everything is also permitted at the 'Easter Apodosis' that is celebrated on a Wednesday. If the consumption of oil (or even fish)[151] is permitted on normal Wednesdays and Fridays during the period of Pentecost, what should then be consumed during the 'Easter Apodosis'?

Non-fasting weeks

The consumption of everything is allowed during the weeks of Easter and Pentecost.

The same also applies during the week of Christmas until the Apodosis on 31st December, when everything is consumed.[152] So when the feast at the Circumcision of Jesus (1st January) was added (in the 9th century), the consumption of everything was continued until the eve of Epiphany.

The consumption of everything is also permitted during the first week of the 'Triodion.' It was a 'reaction' by the Church to the Armenian Bishop Petros' blasphemous views, *"even by the one that is known as Peter the Wolf."* [153]

The consumption of everything is also permitted (excluding meat) during the last week of the 'Triodion.'

ଔ ଓ

---

150 St Theodoros the Studite, ibid, p. 1701
151 St Theodoros the Studite, ibid, p. 1700
152 St Theodoros the Studite, ibid, p. 1697
153 St Theodoros the Studite, ibid, p. 1697-1700

3. THE SICK

Illness is the only reason to break the fast[154] since the purpose of fasting (humiliation of the flesh) is performed by illness. *"We kill the passions; not the flesh."*[155]

What should an ill person consume?

That depends upon how this person fasts, as well as the type of illness. When the ill person fasts by consuming oil, he will need to consume something more than oil. When the ill person fasts by not consuming oil, then he will need to consume oil.

In days gone by where fasting implied dry-rations, the ill person would consume oil. *"It is logical for a person that has been wasted by illness to consume oil."*[156] If they were seriously ill, they could consume fish. However, meat, cheese, eggs, etc., were not permitted even *'at death's door'.*[157]

And that is not all. The sick could break the fast in the afternoon, which implies that they remained hungry until then. And they needed to break the fast in moderation. *"Even the sick that break the fast must not dishonor it* [the

---

[154] *"Except where one is impeded by a bodily illness"* (Canon 66 of Holy Apostles).

[155] Gerontikon, Abba Poimen, 181

[156] St Theophilos of Alexandria, Response X, 'Pidalion', 'Asteros' publications 1982, ibid, p. 670

[157] Constitution, Rallis and Potlis, Vol. 4 p. 487

fast] *through gluttony, for in doing this they shall be censured.*"[158] This may appear scandalous.

"The sick should greet the mother of health."[159] Fasting was considered to be of medicinal value for the sick. In days gone by, Mt Athos Monks would fast for three days, even for tuberculosis, and then recover. Science says the same today.

The Japanese Professor Yoshinori Ohsumi received the 2016 Nobel Prize in Physiology *"for his discoveries of mechanisms for autophagy"* showed the adaptation to starvation as the best medicine for the body's health!

Dr. Norbert Lischka explains that our body burns whatever is redundant when it is cold, and there is no heating. Something similar happens when our body is in a state of starvation (for at least 15-16 hours). *"Our cells begin collecting tumors, viruses and sick or destroyed cells, which are used as 'fuel.' It is an opportunity for the body to get rid of whatever is useless."*[160]

That implies that it is sometimes preferable to remain completely hungry than to eat!

൭ ൏

---

[158] Constitution, Rallis and Potlis, Vol. 4 p. 489
[159] St Basil the Great, Homily 2 on Fasting, P.G. 31: 193
[160] To vima.gr, *"Autophagy heals everything"*

4. THE WIDOW'S TWO COPPER COINS

Christ did not bless the wealthy that donated a lot of money to the Temple, but the widow who had donated two copper coins, because she had donated from the little available to her (Lk. 21:1-4).

We may also lack physical abilities and be unable to observe the fasts fully, so we should offer the 'widow's two copper coins' to the Lord. We should at least fast as much as we are able. For example:

Today it is Wednesday; we may break the fast until midday and then fast, or it is Lent; let us break the fast every weekend or even during the week; let us do whatever we can.

An important "detail": *"Where the fast is broken with pain in the soul because the sick are unable to fast, God perceives this pain as fasting!"* [161] And our reward will not be in accordance with how much we have fasted but how much we have suffered. Paul says: *"They will each be rewarded according to their labor"* (1 Cor. 3:8).

Jesus appeared to Saint Paisios the Great (4th century) and led him into a deserted cave. *"Enter the cave and look upon My agonist,"* Jesus said to him.

The Saint entered the cave and saw an ascetic, who through severe fasting (starvation), was rolling on the

---

[161] Gerontikon. Abba Aio. Abba Isaac the Syrian. Logos 58 & St Symeon the New Theologian, 'The Surviving', Homily 52

ground rubbing his mouth and face into the ground. *"Can you see My athlete? He has been hungry for two days, and you can see how much he is suffering for My sake"*, Christ said to the Saint and added: *"You who have fasted for twenty-two days will receive the same reward as the hermit who has fasted for two days because he has suffered."* [162]

Christ did not say to the ascetic: *"Child, it is enough! You have suffered so much. Eat something, or you will die."* On the contrary, this was model behavior befitting someone who struggles. He was proud of him!

Of course, this does not imply that all the Christians in this world should fast like this Monk! He was a Monk and only had to deal with himself. Christians in society have family, professional and social obligations and should fast as they are physically able so as to fulfill their obligations.

---

[162] Megas Synaxaristis of the Orthodox Church, Vol. 6, 5th Edition, Athens, 1985, p. 263

SECTION IX
WHEN WE DON'T FAST

1. "THAT APPLIES TO MONKS...!"

The Holy Canons do not stipulate different (stricter) fasts for monks and other (less stringent) for laypeople. All of the fasts apply equally to everyone in the Church; to the laity, clerics, and monks. *"Everyone should fast on dry rations during Lent."*[163]

"Surprisingly," laypeople through the centuries have always raised the argument that dry rations apply to Monks. They also said this to St John Chrysostom. *"This does not apply to me. Have I been tonsured as a monk? Am I a monk?"*[164] *"Why do you say this to us who are not monks?"*[165] St John responded:

"Don't say that to me, but tell it to the Apostle St Paul who says: 'do not think about how to gratify the desires of the flesh' (Rom. 13:14). Since he does not say this about the monks, but for those living in the city; the only difference with a person living in the city is that he has a wife; in every other regard he has the same obligations before God. You are accordingly greatly deceived if you consider that different rules

---

[163] Canon 50 of Laodicea
[164] St John Chrysostom, Homily 21 on Genesis, P.G. 53: 183
[165] St John Chrysostom, Homily 7 on Hebrews, P.G. 63: 67

apply to those living in the world as opposed to monks, since Christ did not institute different laws for monks and for those living in the world."[166]

St. John was even stricter in another Homily:

"What are you saying? Are only monks obliged to please God?."[167] "You have been ordered to travel through the narrow gate (Mt. 7:13), and yet you seek rest; You have the commandment to pass through the narrow gate, and you seek the wide gate; What can be worse and more 'crooked' than that? While you are about to ascend to heaven and obtain the Heavenly Kingdom, you ask whether there are any difficulties along the way! Have you no shame? Do you not blush? You do not disappear from the face of the earth!" [168]

"Death occurred because Adam showed contempt for fasting, which is why the earth sprouted thorns and thistles, and our life became painful. See how God is enraged when you show contempt for fasting." [169]

And Saint Basil the Great was also strict with those who violated the divine law of fasting. He said:

"You should fear the example of the rich man. Continuous good living sent him to hell. Despite the fact that he had not been accused of injustice, he burnt in the furnace's flames."[170] "Who has left their bones in the desert and did not see the Promised Land? Wasn't it those who yearned for meat?" (Num. 11:33).

---

[166] St John Chrysostom, Homily 3 on those opposed to monastic life, P.G. 47: 372

[167] St John Chrysostom, Homily 21 on Genesis, P.G. 53: 183

[168] St John Chrysostom, Letter to Demetrios the monk, P.G. 47: 403-404

[169] St John Chrysostom, Homily 5 on Repentance, P.G. 49:307-308

[170] St Basil the Great, Homily 1 on Fasting, P.G. 31:177

Those that remembered the pots of meat (Ex. 16:3) and whose desires turned back to Egypt; don't you fear that example? Don't you shiver that you may lose the future benefits because of your gluttony?" [171]

 C3 ∞

---

[171] St Basil the Great, Homily 1 on Fasting, P.G. 31: 180

2. FASTING IN OUR TIMES

Our world, with its advertisements, TV, the internet, books, magazines, newspapers, 'serves up' whatever is pleasing to our passions and hedonism!

Imagine how difficult it is nowadays for an Orthodox Christian living in such a 'beautiful den of iniquity' to oppose hedonism and be attracted to fasting.

What should Christians do? Should they scorn fasting because they live in such a world? But if Christians break the fasts, then how do they differ from people in the days of Noah who were eating and drinking? (Mt. 24:38). *"Let us not envy the enemies of the Cross by deifying the belly."* [172]

Where there is a will, difficult things become easy, and where there is no will, simple things become difficult.

"The Angels are righteous, not because they are incorporeal, but because they have a will."[173]

---

[172] Triodion, 1st Week of Fasting, Thursday Vespers, Idiomelon of the Aposticha. Phil. 3:17-19: *"Brethren, join in following my example, and note those who so walk...For many walk...and now tell you even weeping, that they are the enemies of the cross of Christ: whose end is destruction, whose god is their belly, and whose glory is in their shame--who set their mind on earthly things"*

[173] St John Chrysostom, Homily 75 on the Gospel by John, P.G. 59:409-410

Even today, there are select Orthodox Christians of all ages and categories who, due to their will, resist the temptations and observe the law of fasting.

They may, of course, consume oil, while in the past, only the sick consumed oil.[174] However, it is also a form of deprivation or distress for the sake of the Crucified Jesus.

There are still secular Christians 'nowadays' that observe the strict traditional fasting, with dry rations!

"Blessed are you who hunger now, for you will be satisfied. Blessed are you who weep now, for you will laugh" (Lk. 6:21). *"Rejoice and be glad, because great is your reward in heaven"* (Mt. 5:12).

There is a well-known Monastery in Greece dedicated to St John the Forerunner (Stemnitsa of Gortynia). It was established in 1167. It is nestled in a mountainside. A woman has once made a solemn promise to travel barefoot from her village to the Monastery and went barefoot, but riding on a horse. Some want to go to Paradise as this woman traveled to the Monastery!

A proverb: *"Paradise is a huge ladder that you can't climb with your hands in your pockets."*

---

[174] St Nicodemus the Hagiorite, Interpretation of Council of the Holy Apostles Canon 69, Pidalion, 'Astir' publications, 1978, p. 95

OTHER BOOKS BY THE SAME AUTHOR
PUBLISHED BY THE SAME PUBLICATIONS

1. Tearful Eyes
2. Christian or an Actor?
3. The World's Final call
4. A Monk's Adventure
5. Confronting the Devil
6. After Death
7. Great Christian Feasts
8. Forty Stormy Years
9. Battles & Passions. Anger, Hatred, Envy
10. Highly Favored One. The Life of Mariam
11. Lion-Tamer
12. Jesus: His Unknown Side
13. St. John Chrysostom. Holy Communion. How & When
14. Heresy is One.

Made in the USA
Middletown, DE
25 July 2021

44613148R00060